POINTS
IN TIME

Points In Time

poems and sketches

2019-23

Dave Donelson

DSDA, Inc.

To Leigh Anna,

May you always be
safe and happy

Table of Contents

A Few Words 1

Now 3

January Gray 4

Train 5

Apology to Carl 6

Singularity 7

Doggerel 10

Our Movie 12

Pain 13

Winter Rain 14

Sonata 15

March 16

Gray Boulders 19

Vernal Equinox 21

Mercy of God 22

Bird Song 24

Ceramic Elephants 26

On This Day 27

Revise, Revise 28

Too Late 29

Before 31

Red Maple 32

Grow, Grass 34

Hands 35

Miracle of the Flowers 37

Aware of Him 38

Funeral 40

Summer Solstice 41

Blast Us Social   42
Sing Me Now   43
Netherworld   45
Bull Frogs   46
Rant No. 523   47
Morning Star   50
Quiet Sunday   51
Lady Godiva's Horse   52
On the Hill   53
Gun Line   54
Garden   56
Rain Came   59
Chill   61
Anticipation   62
Billy   64
Apologies to the Jabberwocky   67
Morning Mist   68
Cabin on the Hill   69
Hoarfrost   72
Center of the Universe   74
Southward   75
The House The Xenon   76
Raise Our Glass   77
Medley of the Carols   78
Snow the Transbender   80
Guitar Picker   81
Farmer Sleep   84
About Dave Donelson   87

A Few Words

I penned my first poem for money in the seventh grade. A buddy paid me fifty cents to write a love poem he could give to his girlfriend. I wrote a few lines in which I rhymed "love" and "turtle dove" and the poem was wretched. It was also intercepted by the teacher when I tried to pass it to my friend. The teacher read it aloud to the class and everyone assumed I was in love with my pal. We were both embarrassed, but I kept the fifty cents.

The poems in this collection were written about sixty years later. They may be wretched as well, but none of them embarrass me very much.

In keeping with the title of this book, "Points In Time," the poems are arranged more or less in chapters corresponding to the passage of time through the year. All were composed from 2019 to 2023, a period of incredible tumult in the world. The COVID pandemic, presidential election, insurrection, impeachments, and foreign invasions filled the media. Closer to home, my wife and I mourned the loss of family members and close friends during those years but also celebrated births, anniversaries, and other milestones.

In the midst of all this, I found some small measure of peace in art and poetry. I wish the same for you.

Now

Now,
A point in time,
Is here and gone.
The pointillist paints with patient dots,
Each considered, miniscule, perfect
Like snake scales
Undetectable in their individuality.
A single hair, one of thousands on the head.
A single leaf, one of millions in the forest.
Each discrete item plays
Its only role.
The whole does not exist otherwise.
Time does not exist
In our logic
Without this single point.
Now.

January Gray

January gray rose the morning
Ashen dawn spread the horizon
Sharp tree limbs faded into blurs

I cry for lost light
Mourn the missing vibrance of the sun
My star is mute behind a cloud

January gray ruled the day
Stole the color from the world
The sky, frozen trees, shivering birds

I dread lightless hours
Hide from the solemn nothing
The book I read rebuffs me

January gray bled the night
Dimmed the stars, erased the moon
The dark end of depthless day

Train

Cold winter morning
Moon not set
Sun not risen
Train sighs along
The platform
Oozing ozone

Hydraulic hiss of
Sliding doors
Warning bells ring
Passengers shuffle
Silence rules
Screen-bound eyes

A hundred strangers
Seated blind
Riding alone
Rock on steel rails
Old joints squeal
Gaskets protest

Engine hums ahead
Wheels grind below
Tickets, please
Motion through space
A marvel of
Ancient physics

Apology to Carl

The fog stomps in
on brontosauran hooves.

It soaks the spruce
and drenches our lungs
before slipping its shroud
over the far horizon.

Singularity

I read today,
In my fine old age,
Of Schwarschild's Singularity.

I can't follow his mathematics,
Much less his convoluted logic,
But what he wrote to Einstein
Turned on a light in my gray head.

Comprehension instantly occurred.

The singularity works simply:
Under infinite compression,
Time becomes space and
Space becomes time.
They interchange,
Meaningless.

How can someone like me—
without a degree in advanced mathematics—
understand this abstract concept?

Answer: I live the singularity.

My age advances and
Time compresses,
Moves faster and slower
Simultaneously.

Doggerel

Every once upon a time
I try to write with words that rhyme.

But when I compile them in a tome
Spelling often blows my pome.

And when I work on perfect meter
I end up scanning lines that teeter.

If I subtly use a metaphor
It stands out like a semaphore.

But wait! Isn't that instead a simile?
You see, they're all the same to me.

Lest I err o'er words archaic
I ne'er allow an apostrophaic.

Poetry is what you make it
Try doggerel and you can fake it

Our Movie

In the movie, everyone is glum.
The actors exchange dark looks
Significant, implacable.
They pretend so well
We grieve with them,
Fear for them,
Flee from their demons.

A slow pan portends
A close closeup clutches
A wide shot establishes

We accept what they pretend.
Is life so grim we must escape?

We act in our own movie.
Glum ourselves, seeking significance,
We pretend in the flickering darkness.
Or do we simply seek anodyne?

Pain

Pain bestows no virtue.
Suffering is not holy.
Martyrs die, nothing more,
Their agony forgotten except
In the phrases of the Pharisees.

We gain no clarity from pain,
No cosmic revelations.
We hurt, we ache existentially.
We learn but one lesson:
Pain is the all, the everything.

We cry for omega.
Make it stop, oh please.
We pray relief for our throbbing soul
And would kill our babies
To seal the bargain.

Pain has a purpose unto itself.
It lives because it lives.
It lives not alone, however.
We writhe with it;
United in its bed.

Winter Rain

Even when winter rain falls
Softly, it is hard.

The concrete cloud spits icy
Arrows, stabbing down.

Raw wind across cheekbone skin
Burned red, scratched and clawed.

Frigid air flays finger tips
Aching, through the gloves.

Stinging sleet invades the eye
Lashes, frozen tears.

Winter bites and kisses lips
Splitting, cracked and blue.

Why do I endure the pain
Of winter and rain.

You are here, and so I too
Stay to be with you.

Sonata

Three deep tones roll in a slow, slow, slow
Arpeggio
Repeated with metronomic measure
In the way the wake of a long-passed boat
laps against the shore.

The third note moves a half tone up, up, back
Making a sixth, a seventh, a fifth.

The bass rolls on slow, slow, slow
Anticipates not the melody
Although you do.
You await me the same way,
But my implacable rhythm will not be hurried.

The right hand will join in its own time
But not before
I will open to you when our time has come.

The left hand plays slow, slow, slow
But it advances time in one inevitable direction
Only when the progression reaches its completion
Will the melody fall lightly down
From the night sky.

When our time comes, we will complete our sonata
With a measured pace bright in the moonlight.

March

March raked us today
Her bitter breath freezes
Our lungs with frost.

March laid her fingers
Over our eyes and
Told us she was sorry

For her winter harshness
And promised to make up for it
With an early spring.

March howled her disdain
For our foolish hopes
And screamed winter in our ears.

Do not be fooled.
March is a liar who laughs
Behind the hand

She holds to hide her true face,
The hand that shades the snow
In the shadows,

The hand that sweeps away the sun
And waves to a gray army
With swords of snow,

The hand that beckons us close
With hope of a soothing stroke
Only to deliver a hurtful slap.

March blew our doors closed
To block our escape
And make us her prisoners.

Wear your short-sleeved shirt.
Bare your pale skin to the sun.
Lick the soft warm breeze.

Bend close to the thawing earth
To smell its promise.
But beware.

See the hyacinth sprouting up
Tender, easily fooled.
March has evil plans

For the green shoots
Drawn upward by her false promises.
March will cough and freeze them

Then pinch them with her icy fingers.
March is a traitor flying the patriot's flag,
A con man bearing bags of counterfeit dollars,

A harlot dressed in a tuxedo.
Today she loves you.
Tomorrow she will stab you.

Gray Boulders

Gray boulders blacken
And reflect the tall hemlock
In winter's mirror.

Tree limbs hang heavy
With rain on tiny needles
Bending branches down.

Grass roots stretch beneath
Sleeping in the rain-soaked earth
Waiting for the sun.

Vernal Equinox

All hail the Vernal Equinox!
The first day of spring!
The last night of winter!

I awoke in my New York bed at 2:37 AM
Eastern Daylight Time,
When the sun shone from directly overhead to a point
Five miles south of Meru, Kenya,
On the Equator.

I went back to sleep dreaming of the time
I first stood on the Equator in Uganda
Where the earth's girdle crosses the Masaka Road between
Nabusanke and Kayalwe,
819 miles from Meru.

I sat on a bench at 2:37 PM,
twelve hours later,
In the sun reflecting from the stone face
Of Kensico Dam.
The sun will set perfectly tonight.

Mercy of God

Salem carries the live mouse
Carefully in her carnivorous mouth
Firm bite with gentle teeth
No escape; no bloody demise

She lays it falsely free
On the blue stone patio
It quivers between her paws
Crouching in fear

The mouse freezes
Paralyzed by the god
Who threatens to devour her
Or not, depending

I know people like the mouse
Fearful of their god's plan
Living with like-minded people
Dreading the one last thing

Bored, Salem paws the mouse
To watch it squirm
In its god's omnipotence
Trying to earn his mercy

Salem turns her head away
The tempted mouse
Darts to freedom in the grass
But Salem reaches in one bound

God's plan is revealed
In the last moment of life
A swipe, a squeal, a snap
An ending sans merci.

Bird Song

Sparrows sip the dew
Warblers graze the grassy lawn
Coffee smells arise.

Sweeping swallows cede
The sky to soft feathered owls
Snuggle off to sleep.

Birds sing dawn to dusk
To celebrate the wonder
Of morning and night.

Ceramic Elephants

A gray ceramic elephant
Stands finial
Atop the iron floor lamp,
Making it special.

Its mate crowns the other lamp
At the sofa's end
Presiding self-important
As if the lamps matched.

The sofa well knows
The shades are identical
But the iron lamps are not.
The elephants lie.

On This Day

On this day, He is risen.
But to what end?
To stab an accusing finger
At the tribe that birthed him?
To flaunt his godhead before
The Mohammedans who come after?
To inspire the witch fires, the gas ovens,
The blazing crosses on the lawns?

He rises to show His Father's love,
They say.
But if His Father loves us, why not raise us all?
Must we, too, don a crown of thorns
And die on the cross
To first demonstrate our love for Him?

We flagellate our dark-skinned slaves
To teach them His name.
Is that not enough?

He arose on this day
Not to free us from our hate
But to bind us closer to Himself
And ensure two thousand years
Of bloodshed in His name.
Let us then color our eggs with dye
And uncage our chicks and bunnies
To celebrate His ascension
From the mire
Where He left us.

Revise, Revise

Every day, write the story of yourself.
Then revise, revise.
Before you even drink your morning coffee,
Spew forth the shitty first draft.
Tell the golden glorious cliches of first kiss with ruby lips,
Of starlit skies on prom night and virginity lost too quickly.

Then revise, revise.
Obliterate your adjectives. Wield a ruthless blue pencil
And annihilate every adverb. Murder all the semicolons.
Free your un-modified nouns to stand tall
And marry unadorned action verbs.
Boil down your life. Render your bacon to its salty singularity.

Then revise, revise.
In the afternoon after your nap, start over.
Tear the morning drivel draft into tiny, tiny tidbits.
Float them in the toilet, then, resolutely flush.
Turn the tablet to a new page of unfilled lines
And fill them up with words profound, words profane.

Then revise, revise.
Craft an appetizer, shrimp with a note of ungrateful children.
Brown a chop for the meat of your life,
Your diaspora from Poughkeepsie.
Pile ice cream on cherry pie, for dessert your twelve steps to
          sobriety.
Take the manuscript to bed and in your dreams,

Revise, revise.

Too Late

I gave my Mom a necklace, but it was too late.
Her birthday was the day before.
    But the day before, I forgot.
    She said nothing, but she cried that night.
I heard her crying behind her closed door.
Worried, I knocked and asked, "What's wrong?"
    "Nothing is wrong," she said. "I am just old."
    That's when I knew I had disappointed her.
A mother, though, is never disappointed in her child.
Her child will always be perfect.
    But I wasn't perfect. I couldn't even get her birthday right.
    I was desperate to make amends, to stop her tears.
The next morning, I tried to dry her tears.
I gave my Mom a necklace, but it was too late.

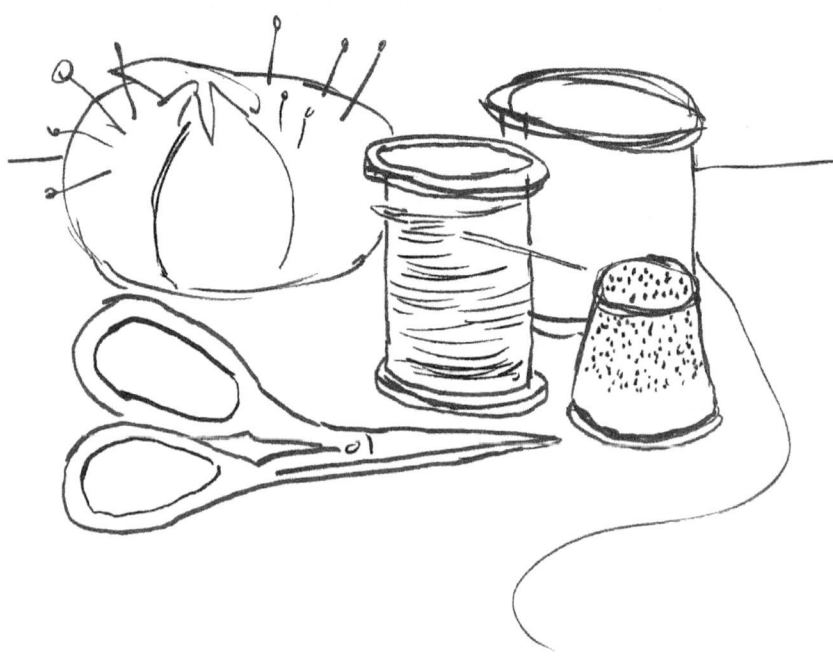

Before

We cannot change the before.
We can only hope to make a future.

Since the past cannot be changed,
Why do we dwell on it so?

Because it is a familiar path,
One whose destination we think we know.

Because it is a comfortable path,
One we walk over and over without fear.

But we can't trust the past.
Our memories of it are not clear.

The historians who wrote it are liars,
Especially if we are those historians.

We say we learn from the past,
but we only learn what we want to learn.

We never want the hard lessons.
Even if we learn them, we ignore them because we can.

Does the past inform the future?
Not reliably.

What happened before doesn't matter.
The only thing that counts is what comes next.

Red Maple

We planted a sapling in a well-dug hole
Mounded the earth around its roots
Wrapped its tender trunk against the deer
Staked it to perfect plumb straightness
Soaked its ground with our sweat
And watched it grow into a tree

A yearling red maple, now
Dangling seed pods with helicopter wings
Unfurling green leaves on pink stems
Spring hues on autumn branches
Warming sun brings the tree to summer
Patiently, we watch delighted,
Assured the tree will take our place

Grow, Grass

Grow, grass, grow!
Green up and gallop to the garden gate.
Grace our ground with your good garment.

Buzz, bee, buzz!
Bumble from bloom to bursting blossom.
Bring their bounty back to your bedmates.

Rise, rose, rise!
Rend the ramparts with raucous red.
Read the riot to your restive retainers.

Hands

The eyes may be windows to the soul,
but the hands express it.
They break, they build, they soothe, they slap.
They mold the earth around the bulb
that will become a pink tulip in the spring.
They snap the beans that will be dinner.
They scratch what itches
and smooth the baby's cowlick.

The fingers of my left hand,
in concert with their opposable thumb,
stop the strings of my guitar while
the right hand strums and plucks them
in mindless coordination.
They don't think, they just do.
Music happens.

You tap your fingers on your knee.
At first, I think you are keeping time to my tune,
but soon see that they don't mark rhythm
but rather your unconscious impatience.
You are too kind to say so,
but you wish my song would end.
My fingers falter and yours, embarrassed,
fly to your face to smoother the "oh!" behind your lips.

My hands set aside my guitar.
You stroke my cheek in apologetic supplication.
With the tip of my forefinger, I trace the blue vein
beneath the skin on the tender back of your hand.

Miracle of the Flowers

The miracle of the flowers occurred today.
Not the blooming of the crimson roses.
Not the blossoming of the blue baptista.
Not the budding of the purple cone flowers.
Not the sprouting of the green pachysandra.
Not the riot of the orange tiger lilies.

Pink plastic geraniums
Variegated ivy
Magenta liatris
White daisies
Green grass spears.

Today, we lifted the wooden window boxes
Onto their perches on the house.
With long reaches from the swaying ladder,
We locked each box onto a cleat.
Two spacers let rain flow out the bottom.
Finally come the flowers on pink foam formations.

The flowers don't grow,
They simply appear.
We don't plant them,
We install them.
From the ground,
They are real enough.

Aware of Him

Over, under, around, and through,
We snake back toward the Garden
To redeem ourselves in the eyes of Him
Who kicked us out for having the audacity
To want to know.

We crawl, we fly, we slither,
Bearing the burden of knowing
That He was wrong in the wrong
For once in his eternal life
To try to deny us our destiny of awareness.

We are not omniscient; neither is He
No matter how strongly he declares it.
We only know what we speculate to be true
And our belief in truth suffices.

He wants no place in our speculation, though.
In his insecurity,
He demands blind, blithering obedience,
Obeisance.

We face Him. We avert not our eyes so
We see Him for what He is.
A tin dictator with mud on His patent leather boots.
A pomposity, a hollow bully,
An embarrassment to His mother.

He rants and blathers.
He blinds little children and
Sucks the breath from the lungs of the dying.

We have now the knowledge
He forbade us to possess.
We find, lose, regret, and rejoice in knowing Him.
We have our revenge
As he hides from our denunciations.

Funeral

The censor puffed its incense,
A smudge pot
On the road to the afterlife.

The priest crunched his cracker,
Quaffed his wine,
Daubed his stained lips with a linen napkin.

He flipped holy water on the casket.
The droplets spotted the wood
No one will see beneath the turf.

The priest waved his hands. We stood.
He waved them again. We sat.
We kneeled, we sang, we kissed our neighbors.

Life eternal is the message.
Eternal damnation awaits
Those who refuse obeisance.

We celebrate the deceased
Who will live forever
Despite what we know about him.

Summer Solstice

For a brief moment yesterday, the longest day of the year,
The sun reached out to touch the Tropic of Cancer
At an absolute ninety degree angle
Like a flag pole plumb to the earth's core,
Gravity reaching under its center to hold it straight up and down.

If the earth were an apple and the sun's rays a pencil,
And you stuck the pencil into the apple at the proper angle
Like the sun at the Tropic of Cancer,
Then pushed the pencil straight through the apple,
It would emerge on the other side at the Tropic of Capricorn
Where six months from now the Winter Solstice will occur.

But the earth is not an apple and the sun doesn't radiate pencils
And we don't weave among the monumental stones on this day
Or dance around the phallic pole with ribbons
Or jump over bonfires holding hands with our future loves.

We watch TV and "huh!" when the meteorologist waxes scientific
About the earth and sun, the apple and the pencil.
All we want to know is, is it summer yet?
The Arctic Circle gets twenty-four hours of daylight today,
But we get equal light and dark and forget it happens.

Blast Us Social

Blast us all a rumor
Of how the world will end.

We will catch it in our teeth
And swallow it whole,

Not hurt by your eye shot,
Impervious to your assault.

Your scream song fades
Before it pierces our ears.

How do you like
Disputations without refutations?

We roll your rumors into a scroll
And stuff it in the sand pit.

We ignore it now,
Waiting for the news, the actuality.

Are you angry yet?
We don't care.

Sing Me Now

Sing me now a song of summer
Morning birdsong, still quiet air
Languid sunrise, cloud wisp sky
A lone worker drives my silent street

Sing me now a song of summer
Midday mayfly, looming heat
Burnished sun glare, cast-iron shade
Tiger lilies strut their orange glory

Sing me now a song of summer
Afternoon miasma, breathless oven
Sol sans mercy, monster eye
Beneath the oak the brindle dog pants

Sing me now a song of summer
Evening pauses, cooling breeze
Strident sunset, red horizon
To my wife I bring a simple salad

Sing me now a song of summer
Blanketing night, earth scents rise
Star-pebbled heavens, stainless moon
The cradle sways to timeless anthems

Netherworld

Not photographing the ocean sunrise,
I lie abed instead in netherworld
Immersed in a half-sleep cinemascope.

A beach cop zooms across the sand riding
Atop a gigantic green zucchini
With balloon tires of pumpkin orange.

He tells me to climb a splintered flag pole
And carefully apply gold nail polish
Across the eagle's finial talons.

An observing seagull enunciates
In mellifluous baritone,
"The bell tolls not for thee, Steven Spielberg."

Crawling slowly down the pole, I answer,
"Tis nobler to suffer the slings of sand
That crackles and crunches beneath your feet."

I receive as pay a weathered sea chest
Bound tight round by rusty chains and padlock.
A blow from a rock reveals my treasure.

Howdy Doody lies in stately repose.
A rosary entwines his white-gloved thumbs
Until sunrise peeps through the window blinds.

Bull Frogs

Bull frogs croak in the black of night
Ribit-it-it, Ribit-it-it, Ribit-it-it

Crickets scrape a one-note fiddle
Scitchity, scritchity, scrichity

Peepers sing soprano chorus
Pree, pree, pree, pree, pree

A damp breeze fills my window
With scent of earthworms and loam.

Mice creep along the garden wall
Big-eyed owls dream of dinner.

A waning moon hangs above
Oblivious to the creatures beneath

The waves of night
Carry us on our musical journey.

Rant No. 523
(randomly numbered)

Three little words that meant so much
I stewed over them for days
Unsure whether to feel insulted or just offended

Or reassured about the human race.
Angry, depressed, or elated?
So few words, so many feelings.

These came in the home center parking lot
From a young bearded man in a plaid shirt
Who uttered them as he stepped from his car

while I loaded bags of mulch into my truck,
Bags that weighed perhaps forty pounds,
Bags I had no trouble lifting and stacking

As I had done many times before in my long life,
Always careful to lift with my legs, not my back,
Working slowly with no muscle-tearing movements.

"Need a hand?"
Said the chipper young man through his full black beard.
I wish I had such hair on my balding head.

"No thanks," I said without thinking. "I'm good."
He said nothing more, just turned and walked away
As I replayed the scene in my mind.

What?
Do I look like I need a hand?
I wanted to shout at his plaid-covered back.

Did you see me struggle? Do you think I'm feeble
Because my face is wrinkled like a pale prune?
The farther he walked, the more snark I muttered.

Driving home, though, I reconsidered.
I should appreciate a young man who offers to help strangers,
A Good Samaritan out to save one old man from himself.

He didn't know I am a perfectly capable geezer
Who throws around forty-pound sacks all the time
As if they are nothing. Just slowly to guard my back.

But enough about me. What about him?
That evening, I wondered if the young man assumes
Every old man is helpless. Old women, too, probably.

All of us with compression socks and age spots.
Even those of us without one foot in the grave
though we may peer over its edge sometimes.

Is there a word for guys like him? An -ist of some kind?
Not misogynist or racist, but bad enough.
Ah, yes, he's a stereotyping agist.

Looks make the label
And the label defines the person—
In this case, me, as helpless.

Or maybe he is really just a nice guy.
I guess I ought to cut him some slack.
After all, shouldn't I be tolerant at my age?

Morning Star

We search the prospect of the dawning sky
And find the answer in the morning star.

When it pierces sharp on the horizon,
We prepare to do the work of the day.

When it obscures its face in misty haze
Our labors will lay heavy upon us.

When deepening clouds stand thick before it,
We savor another cup of coffee.

For labor under the sun is joyful
But gray clouds turn our work to drudgery.

Though it grants no wish, heed the morning star.
It speaks with perfect oracy the day.

Quiet Sunday

Quiet Sunday without lyrics, resting
As my guitar sings whatever song it wants.
I am not the guide; I follow the path
Across the fretted fingerboard to find
A pure tone that sounds long beneath my touch.
The ringing fades into fine tremolo,
Takes a long slow slide to the minor third
Before it falls to diminished seventh
And comes to rest soft on the major root.
The Sunday quiet perfectly resolved.

Lady Godiva's Horse

Lady Godiva rode through Coventry, naked.

The horse she rode was naked, too,

But no one remarks on it.

Her bare butt rubbed his bare back

Her luxurious hair tickled his tender neck

Her fingers tangled in his mane

Her warm breath teased his ear

Yet what of him do the legends speak?

Nothing, not even his name

Even though he, too, walked through Coventry,

naked.

On the Hill

I have been watching you,
Even as you watch me
indulge in carnal pleasure.

I know what you believe,
but you are wrong.
Things are not as they seem.

You may live closer to the sky,
but you are no better
than me, huddled in the mud.

I look different,
but underneath we are the same.
I yearn, I indulge carnal pleasures.

You live above,
but you strive, you weep,
you long for more, just like me.

Your hill does not protect you,
Nor does it hide your sinful thoughts
from me or from your God.

I who lives below see you
for what you are.
I deny your divinity.

Gun Line

A ramrod straight line runs
Clear, uncamouflaged

From
Shameless talking heads
Feeding anger for money
Catering to fear for gain

To
Angry, fear-filled fanatics
Lost in formless rage
Hating all the others

The same straight line runs
Clear, uncamouflaged

From
Fetid lips of fawning politicians
Sucking anger for sustenance.
Dog whistling votes

To
Trigger itched gun worshipers
Waving a black-striped flag
Aiming at anyone different

The deadly straight line runs
Clear, uncamouflaged

Into
The hearts of grocery shoppers
The backs of manicurists
The heads of children
Quivering in classrooms

And

Into
The Capitol Building
Where first insurrectionists
Prepare the next wave
To launch their Reich

Garden

Blue jay cocks one eye
Breeze bends baby breath blossom
Limb left aquiver

Black cat crouches still
Beneath crabapple tree nest
Curls white tip of tail

Why should I marvel
When ducks on clamorous wings
Rise and wheel as one
Forming a flight formation
To grace the next clear pond south

Rhododendron leaves
Thick and green, strong and sturdy
Protect robin's nest

Peony renews
Iris, gladiola, too
Gold finch flits away

Why should I question
The shadow cast by an ant
Falling black on ground
As thick and as dark as mine
Thrown by the same Helios

Chickadee chitters
Thrush steals last safflower seed
Hungry nestlings cry

Bumblebee alights
On aster to sip nectar
Seed falls in winter

Why should I worship
I breathe as the zephyr blows
And it becomes me
When I exhale I am air
I see the sun and am seen

Rain Came

The rain came and went today.
Later it returned, only to leave
Again like an unsure lover.
Each time, it fell soft and steady
To rinse the earth.

The rain smelled not of sky
Or of water but of dirt.
Within each drop swam a mote of dust,
An atom of the loam swept into the sky
By winds from far and long ago.
The mote drew around itself
A cloak of moisture until,
Too heavy to float in the air,
It returned to the earth from which it rose.

Without wind or thunder,
The rain's song soothed the soil,
A lullaby for a restless world,
The pitter of infinite raindrops
Pattering on the ground,
A shush of blessed silence.

Chill

Chill tinges the air
Morning breaths rime my vision
The day begins crisp.

In the brown pin oak,
A dove croons a love song
With tones soft and round.

The ash leaf shivers,
Clutching tight to a dry branch
Holding back autumn.

Anticipation

Anticipation fills my mind to overflow.
What comes next pours in until
Anxiety spills over the lip.

Mental rehearsal digs a channel.
Each repetition deepens a track
That goes one direction
Then starts over and repeats.

The future screens my present.
What I will do hides what I do.
I seek contentment but see uncertainty.

63

Billy

"Feast first with your eyes,"
Billy said when served
A perfectly plated egg
With a sprig of green parsley
Perched on a slice of orange.

"Second, with your nose."
Billy closed his eyes
To taste the full aroma
Of butter on toasted rye
And potatoes on the side.

"Good conversation
Salts the meat," he said,
Then told the sad story of
The waitress with a shiner
Who longs for retribution.

"End with something sweet,"
Billy said, asking
For another slice of toast
With a touch of peach preserve
Before calling for the tab.

"Was she the victim?"
I asked quietly
Over the rim of my cup.
He responded with silence
As if he hadn't heard me.

"You are a cheap date."
Billy winked my way
When the waitress brought the check.
He laid down a Benjamin
And left without his change.

Apologies to the Jabberwocky

We clacked a ferious plaster
And drogged our lachrimone
To somehow brint our skilter
And hide our crine and fone.

We feared the managortus
That pranted on our door.
It skine to cree among us
And brest our glene no more.

So we sklicked down the brender,
Trussed the managortus,
And saved the loocius kender
While questering her turnfuss.

Morning Mist

Morning mist floats soft.
Gentle in the golden glow
Of the back porch lamp,
Dainty deer tracks cross the grass.

Plants bedded this fall
Will hunker through winter,
Roots hard but ready
To drink the thaw
Come springtime.

The morning star hides
Behind the gray horizon.
Fog drapes the tree limbs,
Waiting for the sun to kiss.

Cabin on the Hill

The cabin holds its mysteries close and quiet
Crouching in the woods between giant stones
Near the top of the hill

The cabin ignores creeping vines and mosses
Outlasts grinding ice and blasting wind
Sheltered on top of the hill

The cabin protects itself with isolation
It forgoes a path, makes no chimney smoke
That rises above the top of the hill

The cabin discourages curious trespassers
Grime obscures the glass of unbroken windows
Vandals won't climb to the top of the hill

The cabin hides itself and sometimes me
When I want private silence undisturbed
I retreat to the cabin near the top of the hill

Ye Oya Ryl Zoo

Hoarfrost

Morning hoarfrost white
Covers sleeping grass yellow.
No sun; no sparkle.

Savage dewdrops bite
As skeletal plant spines crack
In the lightless dawn.

Winter grinds away
The sun from the hopeless sky.
Mist freezes on stone.

Center of the Universe

So where then, exactly,
Lies the center of the universe?
Is it here beneath my feet?
Or there, beneath yours?
Are we masters of our space or
Merely its mistresses?

It is said the center does not hold
And it cannot
Because, as it is also said,
The universe endlessly expands.
How could it have a center if
The center endlessly expands?
A growing center has no center
That can be held.

Our center cannot be found.
It shifts beneath our feet.

It is said there are multiple universes.
Do they reside side by side?
Or are they stacked like bricks
One atop the other?
Or do they nestle,
One within the next,
Spooning?

Our universe has no center,
But rather a plethora of centers,
Amorphous with no precision.

Southward

My morning star slides southward
A little more each dawn.
She hides behind the maple
In the corner of the lawn.

The tree was already ancient
When it shaded a gazebo
Where tea was served to baby dolls
While grownups sipped their gin.

But that was always summer.
The day was hot and fine
And the morning star rose bright
Above the horizon line.

Today is autumn, in between,
When each day differs from the next.
Cold, warm, sun, clouds,
Only my morning star knows.

She peeks between the branches
To introduce the sun
That rises cold and brittle
To mark that summer's done.

The House The Xenon

Before there was the house,
There was the land on which it was built,
A hill of gneiss pushed up by tectonic shifts
And razored down by glaciers.

We think the land has been there forever,
But it hasn't. Only for millions of years.
Before that it was ocean
Before that it was magma from the earth's core.
Before that we do not know
what it was or where it was or why it was.

We think we improve it,
But our paltry mining plowing timbering
Drilling bulldozing dam building
Are temporary scars on the land,
Not destined to last any longer
Than the bent-tree huts erected
By the indigenous people
We killed to seize the land.

We don't know anything about the land
The discovery process has just begun
As we create our own demise
Under a cloud of carbon dioxide.
The scientists explore on our behalf,
But findings are not understanding.
An underground vat of liquid Xenon
May have just detected a new particle,
Born in the heart of the sun.

Raise Our Glass

We raise our glass to days gone by,
to days we best remember
in the golden glow of selective memory.
We never toast the other days,
the ones we best forget.

Those we hide in the back room
secure in cardboard cartons,
the worst of them in wooden crates
nailed tightly shut,
the disastrous ones in iron caskets
lined with lead,
buried beneath the floor.

Happy days we praise and polish.
Make them shine like sunrise.
We grow them, stretch them,
make them the whole of our experience,
even though they may have been
just a fleeting moment like
when we first saw our newborn grandson.

So we raise our glass, then drain it,
cherishing the best while drowning the worst.
One glass is enough, though.
A second leads to a third or more,
and only opens the door to the back room.

Medley of the Carols

Oh come, all ye faithful, and deck the halls with boughs of holly.
I'm dreaming of a white Christmas for 'tis the season to be jolly.

It came upon a midnight clear, the first Noel.
A star of wonder over little town of Bethlehem.

Hark the herald angels sing, O Tannenbaum.
Chestnuts roasting on an open fire say God rest ye merry gentlemen.

We three kings of Orient are a joy to the world
And we wish you a merry Christmas.

I wonder as I wander, what child is this?
Away in a manger in a silent night.

Do you hear what I hear?
Yes, I heard the bells on Christmas day.

Silver bells, silver bells!

Snow the Transbender

Snow, the transbender, weighs down
on the house, the shed, the cottage, the barn,
the bushes, the trees, the grass,
the mailbox, the cars, the power lines.
Smothering. Oppressing.

Snow, the bycrusher, piles
on my head, my neck, my shoulders,
my arms, my gloved hands,
my thighs, my booted feet.
Heaving. Hurting.

Snow, the farflinger, blows
across the grass, the road, the sidewalk,
the garden beds, the tree limbs, the roofs,
the chimneys, the gutters, the doors.
Sweeping, Piling.

Snow, the stormcrier, drills
the doors, smacks the windows, tangles the branches,
scours my face, burns my eyes, stings my skin,
pelts the Christmas wreaths, rattles the flue.
Blasting. Blistering.

Snow, the cascadianist, erodes
good will, undermines good nature, rots good intentions,
smothers good ideas, extinguishes good outlooks,
ruins my good temper.
Harming. Hollowing.

Guitar Picker

He's a cross pickin', finger lickin', hoot-n-hollerin' son of a gun.

He never strums when he can thrumb to make his guitar hum.

A drop thumb lick, a pinky flick, the syncopation flies.

Pump handle C, walk to the G, the bass line never lies.

He knows that heaven's empty and the devil don't exist.

So who'd he sell his soul to, to make him pick like this?

His heart beats hard in four-four time, back beat hot and hoppin'.

His first breath sang a treble line that set his cradle rockin'.

He slows it down to ballad time and glides to three-string D.

Then steps it up with twelve bar blues that scream in open E.

He howls the moon and strikes a tune and whines a high sopraner.

He has to play—born that way—from break of day to dinner.

No god made him, no man paid him, his music is his own.

Farmer Sleep

What did they hear at night,
In the small hours of the morning,
When sleep eludes because work intrudes?

Did they toss and turn
To the tune of a boy fox crying for a mate?
Or the hushed whoo of the barn owl
Quieting the rustling mice?

Did they stare at the ceiling in the dark,
Repeatedly plowing the field in their mind,
Rehearsing the labor of the coming day,
Reviewing the work unfinished before sundown?

Did they take slow, measured breaths
Too mimic the sleep that would not come
Because the apple trees needed pruning?

Or lie flat and still to not disturb their spouse
Whose soft snuffles echo the night breeze in the pines?
Did they ever sleep, these toiling farmers of lost centuries?

My head lies on an unforgiving pillow of work to be done.
I channel the tasks over and over
So I won't forget them when the sun arrives.

I do this instead of sleeping,
Not willingly, but because the work demands to be fixed
Into the hours ahead.

I hear not the cry of the fox, but rather the whine of tires
On the highway beyond the ridge,
The relentless hiss of load-bearing wheels,
The endless chorus of commerce.

I dream awake dreams of deadlines and duties,
Lists and measures and corrections to be made and mastered.
I am a sleepless farmer, listening to the night.

A Few Words About Dave Donelson

Dave Donelson's careers as a broadcaster, entrepreneur, writer, and artist have taken him from the jungles of Australia's Cape York Peninsula to the minarets of Riyadh. He's climbed the spire of the Empire State Building, floated the Usumacinta River to the Mayan ruins at Piedras Negras in Guatemala, and photographed the tree-climbing lions and mountain gorillas of Uganda. He's also played and written about golf everywhere from Scotland to Cabo San Lucas, Pebble Beach to Casablanca.

Since 1999, Dave has been a freelance writer and artist and published many books of fiction, non-fiction, memoir, and poetry. His work has appeared in dozens of national and regional print and online publications.

Dave lives in a 300-year-old farmhouse in Westchester County, NY, with his wife, Nora, and an ever-changing roster of dogs, cats, and assorted wildlife. He's frequently found there playing the guitar or banjo.

Books by Dave Donelson

<u>Poetry</u>

Points In Time
Visions of a Certain Age

<u>Memoir</u>

Fathers: a Memoir
The Journal of My Seventieth Year
(four volumes)

<u>Fiction</u>

Hunting Elf
Heart of Diamonds
Blind Curve
Weird Golf

<u>How To</u>

Creative Selling: Boost Your B2B Sales
The Dynamic Manager's Guides
(three volumes)
Slice-Free Golf by Brian Crowell
(editor and photographer)

www.davedonelson.com